M000285421

TO:

_____

FROM:

_____

DATE:

_____

Friendship Is a Happy Place for the Heart: A Book of Encouragement
Copyright © 2019 by DaySpring
First Edition, May 2019

Published by:

DaySpring

P.O. Box 1010
Siloam Springs, AR 72761
dayspring.com

Illustrations by: Julie Phillips
Typeset and Design by: Jessica Wei

Printed in China
Prime: 91625
ISBN: 978-1-68408-677-1

FRIENDSHIP IS a HAPPY PLACE for the HEART

A Book of Encouragement

Really Woolly

Our friendship
is a happy place
for my heart.

Thanking our
Shepherd
for you today!

Time Together

I love hanging out with you!

We may not get as much time in the same pasture as we'd like, but we always pick up right where we left off. Your friendship is comfortable and safe; both secrets and laughter flow freely.

And when things do get really woolly, I know I can count on you to go to our Shepherd for me!

When busy is a badge of honor—as it is in today's world—it's hard to make time for friends. And if friendships aren't nourished by time, they simply don't grow.

We have more ways to communicate than ever before, but we feel more disconnected than ever before, too.

That isn't how God wants His sheep to live! He wants us to live as a flock, bound together by the Spirit and our shared faith in the Shepherd. And He wants us together not only for mutual protection but also to encourage one another with the light and love of Jesus. He wants us to comfort those in the flock who are in pain, love on those who are brokenhearted, and celebrate with those who are taking steps of faith or leaping with joy.

So, my friend, let's get together. I'd love to spend some time with you soon. Just let me know when and where.

*I have you in my heart,
and you are all partners with me in grace.*
PHILIPPIANS 1:7 CSB

WHEN i
tHiNK
of you

(which is pretty often)...

...everything
in my world
gets a little
BRIGHTER.

So glad the Shepherd
put you in my life.

You Brighten My Day

You know how days can blur together, as we do the same things day after day? Get up, eat grass, drink water, eat some more grass, drink some more water, and then go back to the fold.

Well, you have a way of brightening my routine! When you're around, life is sunnier!

Have you ever thought about the fence the Shepherd has put around our pastures? They sure help me feel safe and secure.

So does the rhythm of the world He created. The sun comes up every morning; the moon and stars, every night. The ocean waves keep rolling to shore, and summer becomes fall...becomes winter...becomes spring...becomes summer again.

I like these rhythms.

I also like the rhythm of my weeks and the rhythm of my days. But sometimes, I admit, the peaceful rhythm feels more like a dull routine. Get ready, eat breakfast, go to work, come home, eat dinner, chat a little, crawl into bed...and then do it again the next day—it can be too routine.

I love it when the routine is interrupted by a weekend, with a vacation, or when I get to visit with you! I am grateful for the ways you brighten my days, my weeks, my seasons!

Every time you cross my mind,
I break out in exclamations of thanks to God.
PHILIPPIANS 1:3 THE MESSAGE

WHEN THE SHEPHERD GATHERED HIS SHEEP...

...I'M SO GLAD WE ENDED UP SIDE BY SIDE!

Blessed to Be Friends—
Thankful for YOU!

A Picture of Friendship

When I'm with you, I totally relax. I don't have to put on airs or pretend I'm pasture-perfect. You free me to simply be me! I can share my heart without fearing rejection.

You are a good listener, and always—at just the right time—you remind me of our faithful Shepherd!

We all need friends who accept us, care about us, and point us to the Good Shepherd. We all need friends who don't let anything stand in the way of helping us when life isn't going well and our world feels like it's falling apart.

Maybe you know about the four friends Jesus saw in action. Their paralyzed friend needed help: he needed Jesus' healing touch. Unable to walk, the man lay on a stretcher, and his friends carried him to the house where Jesus was. Unable to enter the door because of the crowd, the men got their friend on top of the roof, dug through it to make an opening, and lowered him to the feet of Jesus. What a picture of friendship!

Like friends on the rooftop, you lift me from the frays of life and help me see my Savior in a whole new way. You've been such a good friend to me, and I hope you know that you can count on me to be there for you!

He fills my life with good things!
PSALM 103:5 TLB

YOUR FRIENDSHIP...

...LiFTS ME UP!*

You bring
*JOY
to my life!

God Brought Us Together

I just watched all the little lambs run toward our Shepherd. Their joy was delightful to see!

The Shepherd makes me joyful, too, and so does your friendship. You seem to know exactly when I need a good laugh, a good cry, or a really good run around the meadow.

You make the Shepherd's love so real to me! I'm glad He put us in the same pasture!

What are the odds? Billions of people live on this planet, and people have lived on this planet for generations and generations. Yet God put both you and me here in this place and at this time. I think He knew we would need each other.

I like thinking about how He brought us together to be friends. Looking back, I see how He was guiding our steps all along. He who created me knew I needed the wonderful you He created. I'm inspired by your deep love for the Shepherd and by your faithfulness in setting aside time to be with Him. I learn so much from the ways you show compassion to our fellow sheep and how you unselfishly listen when you recognize the pain behind the bleating.

I am grateful that our Good Shepherd brought us together and that His Spirit keeps our hearts close.

> God will be the bond
> between me and you.
> I SAMUEL 20:42 THE MESSAGE

FOR you,
from me,
so Happily...

You decorate my life
with the Shepherd's love!

Sharing and Praying

More fun than flying a kite
Even better than a chocolate bite
Sweeter than the breeze blowin' through my hair
Is knowin' that you're there.

Laughin' and gigglin' when we're having fun
Sharing and praying when the day is done
I so enjoy the time we get to spend
And I'm always a little sad when it has to end.

I remember the first time you shared your story with me. As you talked about your mistakes and your pain, I got to know you a little better. What a privilege! Since then we've come to share everything, and I've come to love you more.

The Shepherd truly blesses our friendship, and I know He is pleased when we invite Him into our conversation. Sharing our hearts with each other and with our Good Shepherd as we pray is better for my soul than even the best of chocolate—and that's saying a lot!

You've helped me become more of a prayer warrior than a prayer "worrier." You're teaching me about praying in all circumstances, and your faith in our trustworthy Shepherd's goodness and grace strengthens my faith.

Praying for you is a privilege—and thanking our Shepherd for you gives me such joy!

Thanking God over and over
for you is not only a pleasure;
it's a must.
II THESSALONIANS 1:3 THE MESSAGE

As your day begins,
just wanted to remind you...

God had you in mind
before His first sunrise.

Have a Good Day, Sunshine!

Someone Loves You

Our Shepherd is crazy in love with us!

The very Shepherd who created the universe—who spoke planets, stars, fish, birds, and all the barnyard animals into existence—loves us woolly ones!

He doesn't care that we're not peacock-beautiful, gazelle-swift, lion-hearted, or chimp-clever. He made us, He knows us, and He loves us!

Thank you for making His love for me more real.

Yes, God made us, but it wasn't a cookie-cutter or assembly-line kind of making. According to Psalm 139, God's act of creation was much more personal: He knit each one of us together.

Also very personal is God's knowledge of us: He knows our words before we speak them and our days before we live them.

Now, I can only guess what your future might hold. But sometimes I know exactly what you're thinking. Other times I have a pretty good idea of what you're going to say before you say it.

How did I come to know you so well? According to a recent study, people need to spend at least 200 hours together before they can be considered good friends. I don't think it took us that long, do you? Maybe we're an exception since God planned this friendship long ago.

And He really has been thinking about you for a long time. He knows you better than I do only because He created you, and He loves you more than I possibly can only because... well, because He's God!

Even before He made the world,
God loved us and chose us in Christ to be holy
and without fault in His eyes.
EPHESIANS 1:4 NLT

Dear Shepherd,
we're calling
on You with all
we've got.

When we pray, we're talking
to the Answer—together.

He Hears and Answers

Baaa! Baaaaa!

What a joyful noise our bleating must be when we worship our Good Shepherd and thank Him for His blessings!

Whenever we pray, our Shepherd hears—and He answers. Of course we sheep are happier with "Yes" than with "No" or "Wait." But we can trust that our Shepherd truly is good.

I'm glad you pray for me and trust with me!

Prayer is a privilege, and prayer is a mystery.

What a privilege to be able to approach our holy and almighty God! What a mystery that He hears our prayers, keeps track of them, and answers them perfectly according to His flawless timing.

Truly, God alone is worthy of the adjective "awesome." He is all-knowing, all-powerful, the Creator of the Universe...yet He knows the number of hairs on our heads and the prayers of our hearts.

In Hebrews 4, we're encouraged to go boldly to the throne of God to receive His mercy and to find His grace when we need it. Revelation 5:8 NASB adds that in the throne room of God are "golden bowls of incense" that are the prayers of His people. Our prayers are so fragrant to the Shepherd and so precious to Him that He keeps them near.

So when we pray for one another, may we be mindful of whom we are praying to and how awesome He is. Let's also remember that He loves us so much, He sent His Son to die, paying the penalty for our sin, so we could live with Him eternally. Our Good Shepherd loves to hear our prayers...and to show us His mercy, grace, and love.

He closely attends
to the prayers of God-loyal people.
PROVERBS 15:29 THE MESSAGE

...He'll carry **eVeRY ONe** close to His heart.

So glad to be with you in His care.

Trusting the Shepherd

The lambs didn't see it happen, nor did many of the ewes. But that mountain lion had absolutely no chance of getting a lamb from this flock!

Our Shepherd was right there at the right time with the right weapon. He put his own life at risk to protect us.

I'm glad that when I don't see you across the meadow, I can trust you to our Good Shepherd's love and care.

It was a major showdown! The Hebrew prophet Elijah went head-to-head against 450 prophets of Baal. Whose God would prove more powerful? The world was watching!

As you read 1 Kings 18, you'll see Elijah's confidence that God would send down fire to burn the bull he was sacrificing. In fact, Elijah was so confident that he had four jars of water poured over the bull as well as the wood it lay on. Then he had four more jars of water poured on it. And then four more. The offering was drenched, the wood that would burn it was sopping wet, yet God's fire prevailed. In a glorious, supernatural way, God honored Elijah's total trust and dependence!

Proverbs 3 encourages us to—like Elijah—trust God with all our hearts rather than trusting our limited human understanding of situations. We tend to want to figure things out on our own, then share our plan with God and ask Him to bless it. Prayer doesn't work like that! We are to lay our requests before God, trusting in and depending on His wisdom, power, and grace. And the more often we do this, the more often we see Him come through, and the stronger our trust in Him grows.

What will you trust God for today?

Oh, the joys of those who trust the Lord.
PSALM 40:4 NLT

You're the Shepherd's treasured possession—

and that makes you

PRICELESS.

(I think you're irreplaceable, too!)

One of a Kind!

Sometimes the pasture can be pretty lonely.
That's one reason I'm glad our Shepherd gives
us a flock of friends to share the days, the nights,
the meadows, and the fold.

The Shepherd wants us sheep to love one another,
and we sure get a lot of practice in this flock!

I am very glad He gave me easy-to-love you!

Not only are you easy to love, my friend, but you are a one-of-a-kind amazing creation of our Shepherd—and I am so glad He didn't keep you to Himself. He has given you as a gift to your family and friends. The Good Shepherd knew the ways you would make people feel special and loved. Your smile, your laugh, your encouraging words are all gifts to us who know you and love you!

And there's more good news. The Lord God Almighty—Creator of the Universe, Prince of Peace, King of kings—considers you His own special treasure. Read the verse below. You are an extraordinary treasure, jewel, and prize who He adores.

Throughout history, God has never made another human being like you. He designed you and created you. He has special plans and purposes for you, including sharing eternity with you.

Our Good Shepherd is crazy about one-of-a-kind YOU!

> The LORD your God has chosen you
> to be His own special treasure.
> DEUTERONOMY 7:6 NLT

...are good times
that just take
a little longer
to ripen!

Better Days Ahead

I know what you're thinking! That falling apple is something that would happen to us, right?

We'd be sitting there, enjoying the meadow's breeze—and suddenly an apple would fall and bonk one of us on the head. Of course we'd laugh—and I'm glad for shared laughter.

I'm also glad for shared burdens. Thanks for helping me carry mine. You know how to make me smile when more than an apple has fallen!

We all have days when we wish we had never gotten out of bed. Days when everything seems to go wrong. You run out of hot water in the shower, the shirt you wanted to wear is dirty, you're out of milk, traffic is bad, the project you just completed at work needs to be redone, etc., etc., etc. You get the picture! Sometimes you just want to go home and go back to bed!

Our Good Shepherd knows when you have this kind of day—and He doesn't want you to handle it alone. When the responsibilities and missteps of the day are weighing you down, He invites you to go to Him. He wants to take your burden—your yoke—from your shoulders, give you His easier yoke, and bless you with rest.

The next time you have an everything-goes-wrong day, I hope you'll be able to focus your attention on God and thank Him for making your burden light.

(You can also call me. We can pray on the phone or go grab coffee or do whatever sounds good to you!)

Come to Me, all you who labor
and are heavy laden, and I will give you rest.
Take My yoke upon you and learn from Me,
for I am gentle and lowly in heart,
and you will find rest for your souls.
For My yoke is easy and My burden is light.
MATTHEW 11:28–30 NKJV

Think of you
THANK GOD
Think of
YOU
THANK GOD
THINK OF YOU
Thank GOD

EVERY TIME
I THINK OF YOU—
and I think of you often!—
I THANK GOD
FOR YOU.

I CORINTHIANS 1:4 The Message

Shared Faith

Over and over again I thank our Shepherd for your friendship.

Of course He knew just what I needed in a friend—and He gave me beautiful YOU! I never knew that another sheep in this flock would understand me and like me and love me the way you do!

And both of us are loved by the Shepherd who brought us together to share our faith and a friendship, both of which are rooted in Him!

When I met you and we became friends, I finally understood what it is to have someone in my life who is a kindred spirit. And what a joy it is!

You know me better than anyone else does—and you love me! You understand what I'm feeling when I don't have words. We share the same values, and—most importantly—we share the same love for the Good Shepherd. And because you and I both love Him, our friendship is more than an earthly friendship; ours is a friendship for eternity. What a joy to share with you the glory of heaven and the blessing of seeing Jesus face-to-face!

Can you imagine sitting down with Esther and hearing from her what she was thinking as she approached King Ahasuerus? We'll be able to visit with the apostle Paul and learn more about his travels. When we talk with David and Jonathan, I know we'll be encouraged by those kindred-spirit friends.

And, dear kindred spirit, it's a joy to share the present with you, and it's amazing to think about sharing our eternal future.

I can never stop thanking God
for all the wonderful gifts
He has given you.
I CORINTHIANS 1:4 TLB

Where would we be
without the Shepherd?

Thankfully,
we'll never have to know!

Forever trusting Him with you.

"Always" Means Always

Remember the time we went to the far end of the pasture for clean water? There was our Shepherd!

And then there was the time we went on the other side of the big pond. Our Shepherd was there too!

I like that—wherever we go, He is always with us.

I think He likes being around us as much as we like being around Him!

God is omnipresent: He is everywhere, always.

He is omniscient: He knows everything there is to know.

And He is omnipotent: He is completely powerful.

No, we can't explain or even understand this vastness and divinity. But we can find such peace and hope when we think about our amazing God, who welcomes us as His children.

And He calls us by name and speaks to our hearts. Only rarely do His children hear Him audibly, but all of us can hear inwardly His still small voice.

Good Shepherd, help me hear Your voice more clearly than I've ever heard it before—and then please help me obey. Amen.

> My sheep listen to My voice;
> I know them, and they follow Me....
> No one can snatch them away from Me.
> JOHN 10:27–28 NLT

THE SHEPHERD
CREATED YOU
EXTRA SPECIAL...

...AND WE'RE SO GLAD
HE DID!

One-of-a-Kind Wonderful

Just a few reminders!
God made you one-of-a-kind wonderful!
Our Shepherd delights in giving you, His beloved sheep, the royal treatment!
And He loves you with an everlasting and impossible-to-measure love!
You are special, blessed, and cherished!
The Good Shepherd rejoices over you...
Joyfully * Thankfully * Constantly!
(I also think you're pretty amazing!)

The Bible says that as the Spirit of the Lord works in us, we become more like Jesus, and the more we are like Jesus, the better we reflect His love, grace, and glory. Isn't that an astounding thought?

It can be hard to recognize that kind of growth in ourselves, so let me assure you, my friend, that God's love and grace do shine through you. You reflect His goodness, act with His kindness, and share His joy with the people around you. In all that you do and all that you are, God's glory shines through you!

And I'm thinking that's why folks like to be around you so much. Your faith in God is winsome and attractive. You humbly love others when you listen to them and pray for them, send a note or shoot a text, take a meal or watch the kids. You shine brightly for Him as you live so yielded to His Spirit and so willing to be His hands and feet.

I clearly see our Shepherd reflected in you, and I am so grateful to call you "friend." You are a wonderful blessing to me and to so many of God's lambs.

> And the Lord—who is the Spirit—
> makes us more and more like Him
> as we are changed into His glorious image.
> *II CORINTHIANS 3:18 NLT*

loads
of blessings

That's what's in store for friends
who are friends of the Shepherd!

Thanking God
for you

Whatever You Do

I know you've noticed that wherever we go in this pasture, our Shepherd is with us—and He's blessing us!

He also uses the sheepdog to guide us, and He takes time to be sure our eyes and ears are free of pesky critters. He makes sure we have fresh water and sweet grass.

The Shepherd blesses us in whatever we do and wherever we go—and His love makes me want to bless others.

Let's do something together that will bless others!

What a privilege to be able to bless others as God's representatives in this world! And He is so gracious to provide us with blessings in abundance so that we have the ability to share His love with people we love, with people in need, and through His work in this world.

We can share God's love in pretty simple ways. A smile, a kind word, and a sincere "Thank you!" for the barista when you pick up your morning coffee truly can shine Christ's love into his or her life. When you get to work, your warm "Good morning!" and genuine smile may encourage your coworkers more than you know. If God has blessed you financially, your treating a hurting friend to lunch can be a huge blessing. Likewise, an anonymous gift, through the church, to struggling newlyweds can help them pay their bills and grow their faith in God.

You hear people's words with your heart. You live out in many ways the truth that our Good Shepherd blesses us so that we can bless and encourage others. I am grateful to have as a friend someone who blesses and encourages people wherever she goes. I am grateful for you.

Keep on loving your friends;
do your work in welcoming hearts.
PSALM 36:10 THE MESSAGE

Just wanted to BRiGHten YouR day—

you've BRiGHteNeD
so many of mine!

Not by Chance

Sometimes the Shepherd can be pretty private about what He's up to, but despite that fact, I figured something out.

I've realized that the very best friendships don't happen by chance; they happen by His design. He's the One who gives us friendships that are encouraging...fun and easy... full of laughter...and overflowing with the joy of His love.

I'm thankful today for the special friend the Good Shepherd has given me in you.

Did you know that scientists estimate that you had a one in 400 trillion chance of being born? After all, what are the odds that your grandparents met...had your mother—who met your father and—out of all the men she had ever met—chose to marry him? We can carry out this thought exponentially in either direction: what are the astronomical odds that great-grandparents, great-great-grandparents, and eggs and sperm met to make you? Those scientists rightly conclude that you are a walking, talking, living miracle!

But you already knew that, because you have read Psalm 139:

"You made all the delicate, inner parts of my body and knit me together in my mother's womb. Thank you for making me so wonderfully complex! Your workmanship is marvelous—how well I know it. You watched me as I was being formed in utter seclusion, as I was woven together in the dark of the womb. You saw me before I was born. Every day of my life was recorded in your book. Every moment was laid out before a single day had passed" (Psalm 139:13–16 NLT).

Yes, it's by God's plan that we were born at this time and in this place. Our very existence is totally God's doing, and He knew we would be friends long, long ago.

I thank God for you.
I CORINTHIANS 1:4 THE MESSAGE

...are forever His.

What's in a Name?

The Good Shepherd knows the name of every single one of the sheep in His flock. Our Good Shepherd Himself, however, actually has more names than can fit on this page!

- Jesus
- Savior
- Lord
- Christ
- Messiah
- Emmanuel
- Prince of Peace
- King of kings
- Bread of life
- Redeemer
- Holy One

And the list goes on. And all He is, He is for each one of His sheep. That means you. And me.

According to the Population Reference Bureau's 2018 World Population Data Sheet, roughly 7.5 billion people live on this planet. That's roughly 7 percent of the 108 billion people who have ever lived on Planet Earth. Only our Shepherd knows how accurate these numbers really are.

And He definitely knows every single person living today. In fact, He also knows the name of all the 108 billion people who have ever lived on Earth. All of them. Our amazing God even knows how many hairs are on our heads (Luke 12:7).

Our God is incomprehensibly awesome—and He cares about you and me so very much. He didn't stop with just knowing our names or the number of hairs on our heads. He guides us, He provides for us, He protects us, He blesses us, He rejoices over us.

And He showed us He cares by giving us each other! I'll be forever grateful!

He calls His own sheep by name.
JOHN 10:3 NLT

God's
incredible
goodness...

...shines through you!

Thanks for sharing it!

Our Perfectly Faithful Friend

I've been thinking about meadow life, and I've been watching you treat all of us the way the Shepherd treats us.

I see you coming alongside exhausted ewes with encouragement.

You keep an eye out for lollygagging lambs, and you lovingly keep them from getting lost.

Even the raucous rams respond to your kindness.

What a blessing to have you love me—and the flock—with the Good Shepherd's kind of love!

Imagine being a friend to Jesus, being privileged to share in His three-and-a-half years of ministry...

Maybe around the campfire each person shared why, when Jesus said, "Follow Me," he did. Perhaps Jesus told stories about His Father and about heaven. Jesus may have talked in greater detail about His statement, "I am the good shepherd. The good shepherd lays down his life for the sheep" (John 10:11 ESV), words that gained significance after His crucifixion and resurrection.

Yes, our perfectly faithful and completely sinless Friend lay down His life for us. He took upon Himself the punishment for our sins, and that is love beyond measure, almost love beyond comprehension. The apostle John—one of Jesus' twelve closest friends—wrote, "By this we know love, that [Jesus] laid down his life for us, and we ought to lay down our lives for the brothers" (1 John 3:16).

What a friend we have in Jesus! His death on the cross clearly shows us His friendship and love.

> You have a very special place
> in my heart.
> We have shared together
> the blessings of God.
> PHILIPPIANS 1:7 TLB

*thinking about you
with my heart...*

...remembering you
in my prayers.

The Power of Prayer

There was that night when Lucky Lamb wasn't so lucky, but while we prayed, the Good Shepherd hunted till He found that woolly little guy...

And then when our crazy, wonderful sheepdog broke his leg...we prayed while he hobbled and healed, and now he's as busy and as nippy as ever...

And Granny Ewe got so sick—and we got so sad! But we prayed, and our favorite storyteller got better!

Prayer makes a difference in all matters of the meadow!

Prayer makes a big difference in every aspect of our lives, but we can be reluctant to ask for prayer. We find it risky to even let on that not all is well.

But life is difficult—and the reality is that we can't handle everything that comes our way. The good news is, we don't have to. God gives every single one of us more than we can handle so that we will turn to Him. And why would we ever hesitate when we are:

- Loved unconditionally
- Totally accepted
- Created for a purpose
- Forgiven
- Cherished by God
- Part of His flock
- Able to get wisdom from above
- Welcomed into God's presence
- Able to pray directly to the Creator of the universe
- Promised an eternal home
- Guided and comforted by the Holy Spirit within us
- Crazily loved by a heavenly Father
- Loved by friends we'll know forever
- Blessed to have 24/7 access to the Shepherd

Why do we try to be self-sufficient when we can be Shepherd-sufficient!

Jesus is the One we can trust and rely on to see us through anything. He will not merely show us how to get through something; He will actually walk with us through it. All we need to do is say a quiet prayer.

God...has blessed us with every blessing in heaven because we belong to Christ.
EPHESIANS 1:3 TLB

The Shepherd has
a promise
especially for you...

He's close
to your heart,
and He'll carry
you through.

Praying you feel
surrounded by His love today.

You Are the Shepherd's

You seem a little low, and I realize that words don't always help.

But these are some special words from our Good Shepherd, who stays up night and day, goes before you and beside you, provides for you and protects you. These words just may help—a lot!

I knit you together, Woolly One, just the way I wanted!

I have plans for you in this meadow, and these plans are for your good.

Nothing can separate you from My love! Nothing!

I collect your tears in a bottle...and I bring beauty out of ashes.

I bless you so you will be able to bless others inside and outside the flock.

And I have prepared a heavenly, eternal sheepfold for you!

The Shepherd loves you so much. And I do too.

As our woolly friends were saying, you are the Shepherd's. But you are more than a sheep in His flock—although that is blessing enough.

You are, in fact, also an heir of God, who is the King of kings (Galatians 4:7). You are therefore a joint heir with Jesus (Romans 8:17). Think about that truth!

You are a daughter of the King, and in His kingdom we find ready access to limitless love, joy, peace, patience, kindness, goodness, faithfulness, gentleness, and self-control.

Life in God's kingdom also means that He shall supply all your needs according to His riches in glory by Christ Jesus (Philippians 4:19 NKJV). He will supply not some or part or a portion or a little or half or three-fourths of what you need. Your heavenly Father—who is also King of kings—will supply all that you need!

The King will take good care of His daughter because He loves you. (And I do too!)

> I will be your God through all your lifetime...
> I made you and I will care for you.
> I will carry you along and be your Savior.
> ISAIAH 46:4 TLB

THANKS!

My heart's overflowing with
GRATEFULNESS,
BLESSINGS,
GRATITUDE,
THANKFULNESS,
AND
APPRECIATION
to the Lord for you!

Thanking God for You!

I know what you're thinking!

First you were surprised to read those words, but now you're standing on your side of the pasture thinking, "Why is she thanking me?"

Well, it's not because of anything you've done, even though you're always doing nice things for me!

I'm thanking you just for being you! And I thank our Good Shepherd, the Giver of all good gifts, for sending me such a faithful and faith-filled friend...for sending me you!

Developing an attitude of thankfulness, whatever our circumstances, is a sure path to choosing joy in this life. Granted, life gives us plenty of reasons to be sad and genuine reasons to grieve, and we all have days when nothing seems to go right. But finding something to thank the Shepherd for may be what God uses to lift our spirits on the darkest days and despite the heaviest burdens.

Have you ever thanked God for butterflies, green grass, blue skies, fluffy clouds, pine trees, dogwood trees, azaleas, rainy days, sunshiny days, cool breezes, beautiful sunrises and sunsets, ocean waves, majestic mountains, foggy valleys, or puddles to splash in? How about a baby's pudgy cheeks, a friendly smile, your eyes that see, your ears that hear, your legs that walk, a room full of laughter, or the ability to speak?

The more I think about it, the more there is to be thankful for! Maybe some of these things are on your list: a roof over your head, food to eat, clothes to wear, a job, family and friends who love us, their hugs, prayer, God's Word, brothers and sisters in Christ, the satisfaction of a job well done, passing faith on to future generations, and simply having coffee with a friend. This list can go on and on.

What are some other things you're going to thank God for? I know! I'm going to thank Him for you!

May you be blessed by the LORD.
PSALM 115:15 NLT

Asking God to turn
your rainy days...

...into showers of blessings!

Showers of Blessings

Rainy days can be so cozy when we huddle in the sheepfold with the rest of the flock. We listen to the rain and Granny Ewe's stories. We imagine how sweet the grass and how clean the air will be after the rains.

But sometimes rainy days can be lonely even when we're huddled with the flock, and I'm sorry. I know you know the Good Shepherd loves you.

I love you, too, and I'm praying for you—and looking forward to celebrating the return of sunshiny showers of blessings in His perfect timing.

You, my friend, are used to my random thoughts....

So...Jesus asked the Father to shower us with blessings. Just how many blessings might that be? I googled to find out how many raindrops are in a shower. The closest answer I could find is the fact that there are 412,700,000 raindrops in a cubic foot.

So if God showered us with a cubic foot of blessings that just might mean 412,700,000 blessings. That is definitely blessing in abundance from the One who can "shout to the clouds and make it rain" (Job 38:34 NLT)!

And since our God can shout at a cloud and make it rain, don't you suppose He could shout at a situation and cause blessings to come from it? He is more than able to bless us whatever our circumstances!

I'm glad He blessed me with your friendship!

May God our Father shower you with blessings
and fill you with His great peace.
COLOSSIANS 1:2 TLB

THIS
IS THE DAY
THE LORD
HAS MADE...

...AND iT's
YOURS!

You Are Loved!!

Building Up
Each Other's Faith

Sometimes we silly sheep wander off into brambles, straying from what the Shepherd's Book teaches and listening to voices that don't reflect the truth. Our drifting from His ways saddens the Shepherd, but He took this risk when He gave us the freedom to choose.

What pleases our Shepherd is our grazing in fields that He has watered. He also wants us guided and protected by shepherds who truly love Him and who teach from His Book.

You know, one reason God made us friends just may be so we can build up each other's faith in Him. Let's help each other be sure we're drinking the fresh water and grazing in the green pastureland of our Good Shepherd's truth. We don't want brambles in our souls!

90

Throughout the New Testament, followers of Jesus are told to love one another. One way we can do that is by helping each other stay grounded in God's Word and growing in our faith.

When we don't understand a passage, let's simply ask someone more knowledgeable. When we see someone straying from the Truth, may we humbly offer biblical correction.

From generation to generation people have encouraged one another in their faith life, and from generation to generation they have passed along their faith to family and friends.

I want you to know that you are passing along your faith when people see Jesus in you. You encourage them with your kind words, lift them up with your thoughtful acts, and brighten their world with your joy in the Lord. And I know you're ready to share the gospel when they ask you what's different about you.

Keep shining brightly for your Good Shepherd! Your daily faithfulness pleases Him and blesses others—including me!

Your love has given me much joy.
PHILEMON 1:7 NLT

WHEN WE LOOK to tHE SHEPHERD
foR OUR eVERY NEED...

...it's Nice to KnOw He's aLReaDy Looking out foR us.

Keeping you in my prayers.

He Watches Over You

Have you ever noticed that our Shepherd seems to always be around?

No matter where we are in the pasture, whether we're on this side of the creek or the other, whether we're standing in the middle of the flock or we've wandered off a little way, our Good Shepherd is always nearby.

I'm beginning to believe He never sleeps! What a blessing to have our Good Shepherd guarding us 24/7!

Have no fears or worries—
Simply be at rest,
Trusting in your Father;
He knows what is best.
Everything He's promised
He will surely do—
God, who sees the sparrow,
Watches over you.

This simple poem by Roy Lessin offers us profound and powerful truths about our Shepherd. We truly don't need to worry or fret. Instead, we can choose to rest and trust our heavenly Father who absolutely knows what is best for us. Since we ourselves don't even know what's best for us, resting and trusting Him is an excellent and wise choice.

Mr. Lessin also reminds us that God will do "everything He's promised." And how many of His promises do we find in His Word? According to Bible Gateway, God has made 5,467 promises. Many of His promises are conditional: He will always fulfill His end of the promise every time, but we will not receive the blessing when we disobey.

God's love, however, is unconditional. Your heavenly Father watches over you 24/7, and He wants to walk with you through your days. Enjoy every time you check in with Him. He certainly does!

The eyes of the LORD watch over those who do right,
and His ears are open to their prayers.
I PETER 3:12 NLT

God crafted

something wonderful

in you...

...a fabulous friend
for me.

SO THaNKFUL
for His Amazing
Workmanship

God's Marvelous Creation: YOU!

"In the beginning, God created the heavens and the earth."

I love when Granny Ewe tells this story. "And He made the light, and it was good.... And He made the stars and the moon, the green grass and big ponds, the sheepdog and us sheep. And He made everything good. He delights in what He made"—and that includes most excellent you!

I'm so glad He brought us together in this big, beautiful world of His!

In Psalm 139:14 HCSB the psalmist says: "I have been remarkably and wondrously made." Here are a few facts from *National Geographic for Kids* that will show you something about how remarkable you are:

1. Laid end to end, an adult's blood vessels would circle the earth's equator four times!
2. In the average person's life span, the human heart beats over three billion times.
3. Information zooms across nerves at 400 kilometers per hour.
4. Scientists estimate that the human nose can recognize a trillion scents.
5. Human teeth are as strong as shark teeth.

Scientists also believe that we have up to 70,000 thoughts in a day; that a human eye can identify up to 10 million colors; and that our brains' long-term memory can hold as many as one quadrillion (1 million billion) separate pieces of information over a lifetime.

Did you know that scientists also believe that every human thumbprint and every human voice is unique and different? Why would God do that? Would any of us care if our thumbprint were the same as someone else's? Probably not. But our Maker is infinitely creative, and He clearly delights in the process. He truly has made us remarkable and wondrous!

His radiance exceeds anything in earth and sky;
He's built a monument—His very own people!
PSALM 148:13, 14 THE MESSAGE

Thought
you might
need a little
pick-me-up
today...

...so I prayed for you.

Is It Fellowship or "Fellowsheep"?

The Shepherd likes it when we sheep hang out together. He has a fancy word for it that I can't quite remember.

He likes it when we listen to His voice together, when we sing together, when we pray together. Oh, the word is coming to me.

He really likes it when we celebrate His love—the way you and I like to do, just the two of us! Oh! The word—but is it *fellowship* or *fellowsheep*?

God loves when the people He created spend time together. Whether we're worshipping on a Saturday night or a Sunday morning, discussing the sermon in a small group, praying for God's work around the world, serving at the homeless shelter, or cleaning up the church grounds, God smiles.

Our fellowship with other believers reflects the mystery of divine fellowship: God lives in constant communion and fellowship within His triune Self—Father, Son, and Holy Spirit. Wanting us to know that kind of joyous connection, God calls us to meet together regularly, to encourage one another to do good works, to serve one another, and—most importantly—to love one another. After all, the world will know we are Christians by the way we love.

Scripture also says, "If we walk in the light as He is in the light, we have fellowship with one another" (1 John 1:7 NKJV). May we walk so consistently in our Shepherd's glorious light that others are attracted by His beauty and want to know Him too.

Share each other's burdens,
and in this way obey the law of Christ.
GALATIANS 6:2 NLT

Out of alllll His CREATION...

...He loves His sheep the most.

Just wanted to remind you
how special you are to Him—
and to me.

Praying for you

The Shepherd's Good Creation

Of course I've been thinking of you.

And this is what I thought: When God created you and then looked on you with eyes full of love, I am sure He stepped back, smiled, and proclaimed, "It is good!"

When I look at you, I, too, see the goodness of His creation. And the goodness of our Shepherd.

I am so grateful for our Good Shepherd, for the gift He has given me in you, and for the ways He uses you to grow my faith and spur my obedience. Through you, He encourages me, loves me, and teaches me about Himself and about living for His glory. Beauty is more radiant, joy is richer, and pain is easier to deal with when I share life with you.

Being the true friends we are, we celebrate the good things together, and we grieve the sad, the hard, the lonely together. We also sharpen each other, taking turns being the sharpener and the sharpened.

Oh, occasionally we hurt one another, but never on purpose. When that does happen, we imperfect and bumbling sheep are grateful that the basis of our friendship is love and that love enables us to forgive and receive forgiveness.

And the foundation of our love is both our love for Jesus, the Good Shepherd, and His love for us. Nothing is more solid than that!

So may God continue to use us in each other's lives—with vulnerability, kindness, and grace—to spur one another on toward love, toward courage, toward goodness, and toward our God who is madly in love with us.

Try to realize what this means—the Lord is God!
He made us—we are His people,
the sheep of His pasture.
PSALM 100:3 TLB

The Shepherd has a great
weight-lifting program...

...no matter how heavy our cares—
He's faithful to lift each one!

Hope Your Heart Feels Light
in the Promise of His Love Today

Cares, Begone!

Trust your Shepherd once again
    as you've trusted Him before.
He'll show to you His goodness
    and His faithfulness once more.

Rest in Him your problems;
    give to Him your care.
When you're in your greatest need,
    just know that He is there.

A friend recently asked me whether I am a worrier or a warrior. Do I respond to tough circumstances or bad news or sudden changes with worry or with prayer? These questions really challenged me.

As I thought about these questions, I remembered hearing that worry is actually a form of fear and that a good acronym for fear is False Evidence Appearing Real. If I choose worry, I can easily get worked up about something that will never even happen.

Another reason worry is a bad choice is because the Shepherd loves us deeply. He wants us to leave our worries and cares at His feet. He wants us to trust Him wholeheartedly and be absolutely confident that He can and will take care of us.

Is any situation we face too hard for God? Is any problem that keeps us awake at night too complicated for Him to solve? Is any situation too complex that He can't direct our steps and guide us through? No, no, and no!

Whatever you're facing, the Shepherd's got this!

Let Him have all your worries and cares,
for He is always thinking about you
and watching everything that concerns you.
I PETER 5:7 TLB

From our
WORRIES...
to our
WORSHIP...

...it's so good to bring
   it all to the Shepherd.

TRUSTING HIM

with you today.

He Is All We Need

What words would our Shepherd use to describe us?
Woolly, of course. But maybe prone to wander, easily
distracted, defenseless, needy. Now look at the list
of words that describe our Good Shepherd. What a
blessing to be in His flock!

- Way
- Friend
- Wisdom
- Hope
- Security
- Life
- Protector
- Shelter
- Guide
- Strength
- Joy
- Provider
- Shield
- Help
- Defender
- Peace
- Counselor

Again, what a blessing that the Good Shepherd
is our Shepherd!

Good friends...

Are good for each other. *"Two are better than one because they have a good return for their labor"* (Ecclesiastes 4:9 NASB).

Give each other a case of the smiles at just the right time. *"We who had sweet fellowship together..."* (Psalm 55:14 NASB).

Listen to each other. *"Better is a neighbor who is near than a brother far away"* (Proverbs 27:10 NASB).

Share their hearts with each other. *"A sweet friendship refreshes the soul"* (Proverbs 27:9 THE MESSAGE).

Know when to handle each other with care. *"A friend loves at all times"* (Proverbs 17:17 NASB).

Know when the other needs a kick in the pants! *"Faithful are the wounds of a friend"* (Proverbs 27:6 NASB).

Make the hard times easier. *"There is a friend who sticks closer than a brother"* (Proverbs 18:24 NASB).

Make the good times great! *"O magnify the LORD with me, and let us exalt His name together"* (Psalm 34:3 NASB).

Are a gift. *"Every perfect gift is from above"* (James 1:17 NASB).

So blessed to have you as my friend! I'm so thankful the Good Shepherd brought you into my life.

I will keep on hoping for Your help;
I will praise You more and more.
PSALM 71:14 NLT

So GLAD we
CAN SHARE WiTH
EACH OTHER...

...AND WITH OUR
SHEPHERD.

Praying for you!

Call to Me!

We are blessed to be able to call to our Good Shepherd any time, day or night. We can call to Him to chat for a bit, pray for a while, or sit with Him quietly. (I'm also blessed to be able to call you any time, day or night!)

Knowing the Shepherd's round-the-clock attention and care makes life in the meadow a little bit of heaven on earth.

He is a good, good Shepherd!

It's like having our Shepherd's number on our phone as one of our favorites—and knowing that He will always pick up! He is always there, always ready to listen, always ready to answer. Our Shepherd Himself put it this way:

> *Call to Me, and I will answer you,*
> *and show you great and mighty things,*
> *which you do not know.*
> (JEREMIAH 33:3 NKJV)

Other versions of Scripture say that our Shepherd will tell us "marvelous and wondrous things" (THE MESSAGE) or "remarkable secrets" (NLT). We truly have a direct line to God. We call...He answers...and He may just let us in on some "great and mighty things."

Those "great and mighty things" may be different for each of us. After all, God knows the plans He has for each of us. He also knows our hearts—our deepest hurts and needs and desires. So maybe next time you're having a private chat with the Shepherd, ask Him whether He has anything to share with you. Then take time to sit with Him and listen.

Just like when you and I enjoy each other's company in comfortable silence, you'll be blessed even if He doesn't reveal a remarkable secret. You'll be blessed by spending time in the warm, quiet presence of your Good Shepherd.

I pray for you...that God who gives you hope
will keep you happy and full of peace.
ROMANS 15:13 TLB

If I could pick
a *perfect* day...

...I'd ask God to give it to you.

A Good Day

Under the Shepherd's care, you and I can see reasons that every day is a good day.

Sometimes we can sleep in, enjoying warm and fuzzy dreams. Or we can meander through the meadow to the stream, enjoying its peacefulness. We can frolic in the pasture with the lambs, enjoying their carefree sense of fun. We can meet at sundown to read the Shepherd's Book and pray together.

Yes, under the Shepherd's care, we can find good in every day!

I found this letter, my friend! I hope you got a copy, too, but if not, I want to share mine.

Good morning. This is God. Just calling to confirm the contents of the delivery I arranged for you. You should have received the following:

- One custom-made day to rejoice and be glad in (Psalm 118:24).
- New mercies that reflect My great faithfulness (Lamentations 3:23).
- My divine power for all things pertaining to life and godliness (II Peter 1:3).
- The good works I've prepared beforehand for you to walk in (Ephesians 2:10).
- My joy that gives you strength (Nehemiah 8:10).
- My peace that passes all understanding (Philippians 4:7).
- My grace that is sufficient for your time of need (II Corinthians 12:9).
- A way of escape for every temptation (I Corinthians 10:13).
- My precious and magnificent promises (II Peter 1:4).
- A hope that will not disappoint (Romans 5:5).
- My everlasting love (Jeremiah 31:3).
- My very presence with you (II Corinthians 3:3–4).

Special note: This package does not include a record of your sins. That was nailed to the cross. Blessings!

> This is the day the Lord has made.
> We will rejoice and be glad in it.
> PSALM 118:24 NLT

Even when we
can't see Him...

...He is with us.
His love, peace, and
joy to you today.

The Free Gift

Remember that the Shepherd is with you.
He is with you as your Friend, to support you...
as your Shield, to protect you...
as your Strength, to sustain you...
as your Life, to enrich you.

(I'm here for you too!)

God so loved the world that He...came to change it by changing the people in it. The change would not be political, environmental, or economic; it would be a change of the human heart.

And this heart change would come as a gift. The gift did not come in fancy wrappings, nor was it only for the wealthy, the powerful, the popular. This gift would be available to anyone who was humble enough to receive it.

The Gift lived among potential recipients. The Gift was love, God's love in the form of a Man we know as Jesus, as Savior and Lord. Each person who welcomes Him experiences the change that only His love can make.

When we receive God's Gift, our hearts know peace and joy and the promise of this love extending into eternity. We thank You, sweet Shepherd, for Your love beyond measure, Your peace that passes understanding, and Your joy unspeakable in our lives.

And I thank You for my friend to share it with.

> The free gift of God is eternal life
> in Christ Jesus our Lord.
> ROMANS 6:23 ESV

...just can't find a word
better than His
to tell you
how thankful I am for you!

A Heart of Thanks...

For little things like clover, for big things like fences, for all things in the meadow—we can thank our Good Shepherd!

We can also thank our Shepherd for being ever present, always faithful, and unconditionally loving. We may not always see His fingerprints—we may not always be looking!—but He is in every circumstance and each moment of all our days.

When we choose thankfulness, we are on the Shepherd's path to true joy.

And that is a beautiful place to be.

(I thank Him, too, for the friendship and joy we share!)

...To My Friend of the Heart

A friend of the heart brings joy like...*a surprise bouquet of flowers and your favorite chocolate.*

A friend of the heart helps you...*soar higher and reach new heights.*

A friend of the heart knows...*how to bring out the best in you—and exactly the moment you need a reminder that you're loved.*

A friend of the heart...*is there for you when you need her and listens when you need an understanding ear.*

A friend of the heart helps you...*keep pressing on when life gets turned upside down and remember what truly matters in the meadow.*

A friend of the heart is a gift from the Shepherd's heart. I am grateful for you, my friend of the heart.

> Every time you cross my mind,
> I break out in exclamations
> of thanks to God.
> PHILIPPIANS 1:3 THE MESSAGE

the LORD's love
never ends; His mercies
never stop. they are new
every morning.

LAMENTATIONS 3:22–23 NCV

Just a little reminder
that you are in God's care
and many prayers today.

Loved and Enabled to Love Others

Whether life right now is really woolly or all is well in the meadow, it's good to be reminded that our Good Shepherd cares about every detail of your life....

- He provides for you in the same way that He provides for the birds of the air and the flowers of the field—and He'll never stop (Matthew 6:25–32).

- He knows what you're thinking—and He loves you anyway! (Psalm 139:2).

- He knows every hurt in your heart—and He will be your Comforter (Psalm 34:18).

- He has written your name in the Book of Life— and He will never erase it (Revelation 3:5).

- He rejoices over you with singing—and He keeps you as the apple of His eye (Zephaniah 3:17; Psalm 17:8).

(Please remind me when I forget!)

Not only does the Shepherd care about every detail of your life, but He also calls us to care for one another. Throughout Scripture we find divine instruction on how to treat one another—and of course this is good instruction for being a friend. Take a look at these!

- Love one another (John 13:34).
- Encourage one another (Hebrews 3:13).
- Be kind to one another (Ephesians 4:32).
- Serve one another (Galatians 5:13).
- Fellowship with one another (1 John 4:7).
- Pray for one another (James 5:16).
- Accept one another (1 Peter 3:8).
- Care for one another (John 15:12).
- Bless one another (Genesis 48:20).
- Build one another up (1 Thessalonians 5:11).
- Live in harmony with one another (Romans 12:16).
- Greet one another (Romans 16:16).
- Do good to one another (1 Thessalonians 5:15).
- Look after one another (Hebrews 12:15).

They say the best way to have a friend is to be a friend. You are a wonderful friend! It's a blessing to be your "one another"!

God cares...right down to the last detail.
JAMES 5:11 THE MESSAGE

Wait for it,
Wait for it...

God's beautiful blessing
of YOU
has bloomed
in thankful hearts
like mine.

Waiting with Hope

Wait for it...Wait for it...Another minute or two....

Don't you just hate waiting? I do! Especially when I have to wait to spend time with you!

Life is busy and rich and full for both of us. And that's exactly why we need friend time away from the flock. You keep me grounded, you remind me of the Good Shepherd's faithfulness, and you love me whether I just got sheared or I'm super shaggy!

I just love Romans 15:13—all its parts and the verse as a whole.

I PRAY THAT GOD, THE SOURCE OF HOPE...
Our Good Shepherd is a God of hope! I'd much rather serve Him than a God of despair, a God of fear, or a God of "It ain't gonna happen."

WILL FILL YOU COMPLETELY WITH JOY AND PEACE...
Our God of hope fills us with joy and peace, not bitterness and backbiting. And He doesn't give us just a little joy and peace. He fills us completely.

BECAUSE YOU TRUST IN HIM...
Why wouldn't we trust the God who blesses us with hope and joy and peace?

THEN YOU WILL OVERFLOW WITH CONFIDENT HOPE...
Just as our gracious God fills us completely with joy and peace, He also generously fills us with hope to the point of overflowing.

THROUGH THE POWER OF THE HOLY SPIRIT.
And these blessings of hope, joy, and peace come from the Holy Spirit, the greatest power in the universe, the power that raised Jesus from the dead.

My friend, I pray that you are filled with the Good Shepherd's joy, basking in His peace, and overflowing with His hope!

I pray that God, the source of hope, will fill you completely with joy and peace because you trust in him. Then you will overflow with confident hope through the power of the Holy Spirit.
ROMANS 15:13 NLT

We could knit our socks off
and never come close
to the Shepherd's
wonderful
creation.

He created you!!!

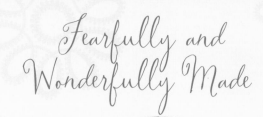

Fearfully and Wonderfully Made

How many hundreds, thousands, maybe millions of tiny hairs do we have on our bodies?

I don't know either—but when I was reading the Shepherd's Book the other day, I saw that He knows how many hairs each one of us sheep have, from muzzle to tail, from hoof to head! Really, it's true!

Our Shepherd knows EVERYTHING about us! And you know what I like best about the way He made you? EVERYTHING!!

It really doesn't matter to me how many hairs you have, my woolly friend. I like the whole wonderful package!

Did you know that scientists estimate the average human body to have somewhere between 30 and 40 TRILLION cells? And according to Scripture, God knit all of those together.

With that truth in mind, think about the times we look in the mirror and say, "Oh, I wish this part of me were different" or "Why can't I look like so-and-so?" The next time those thoughts come to mind, remind yourself that God knit you together. You are His one-of-a-kind, handcrafted creation...and every single one of His creations is WONDERFUL!!

Now, what if everyone in the world looked at everyone else through that lens? What if we saw each other the way God sees each person, as His beautiful, amazing, handcrafted, beloved creation?

I have no trouble seeing you as the Shepherd's beautiful, amazing, handcrafted, beloved creation. May He help me see others like that too.

> You made all the delicate, inner parts
> of my body and knit them together....
> Thank You for making me so wonderfully complex!
> It is amazing to think about.
> PSALM 139:13—14 TLB

...YOU!

Just wanted you to know the Lord brought you to mind.

Thinking of You
Makes Me Smile!

Maybe you've had it happen.

You're in the middle of some afternoon grazing,

rather preoccupied by ram and lamb issues...

when suddenly the thought of someone special offers a pleasant interruption.

What a blessing she is to you!

That simple fact lifts your heart and

makes you smile,

and you find your heart overflowing with thankfulness to your Good Shepherd.

That's me...thinking about you...and asking the Shepherd to bless your day.

In Hebrews 3:13, we are told to "encourage each other daily" (CSB). In I Thessalonians 5:11 (CSB), we read, "Encourage one another and build each other up." We also learn in Proverbs 12:25 that "Anxiety in a person's heart weighs it down, but a good word cheers it up" (CSB). Clearly, these writers knew that there can be storms in the meadow and tensions in the flock, that life can be tough and we can get discouraged. The writers recognized that we all need encouragement from time to time.

And God calls those of us who love and follow the Good Shepherd to encourage one another. God wants us to speak truth to those we know are discouraged and remind them that God has overcome the world (John 16:33) and that He has plans to prosper them and not to harm them (Jeremiah 29:11).

Encouragement can take many forms, ranging from words to a meal to childcare to underwriting a counseling session, to prayer—the list is endless, and those items can cost us. Yet when we encourage one another, our obedient sharing of God's love gives Him glory.

Our Good Shepherd smiles as we live out I John 3:16—"This is how we have come to know love: He laid down His life for us. We should also lay down our lives for our brothers and sisters" (CSB).

(Thank you, my friend, for the ways you have encouraged me.)

> I always thank my God for you and
> for the gracious gifts He has given you.
> I CORINTHIANS 1:4 NLT

...will the Shepherd
leave you!

And I'll stick close too!

Good News for Today— and Always

When the dark storm clouds roll in, the wolves howl, or the flock isn't getting along well, we are so blessed to know that the Shepherd is absolutely in charge and in control! Just as you often remind me, I'm going to remind you...

He is beside you,
behind you,
before you,
and for you!

No doubt about it, no way around it, God's plan for you is good, His power is great, and His love will never fail you, my friend. I'll remind you of these truths as often as you'd like—and please remind me.

You're living in the shadow of storm clouds, wondering if they will rain down more loss and pain. That's a hard place to be, and I'm so sorry you are in that season now.

Know that I'm praying for you as you walk in those shadows. I'm praying with all my heart that...

- The Lord will send individuals who offer genuine comfort, even silent comfort—individuals who will let you be who you need to be right now.

- You are hearing from the Lord in your heart of hearts as He speaks words of His tender love, His strong love, His unfailing love for you.

- You can choose to believe that the Lord—your Good Shepherd—is miraculously creating something beautiful from the ashes of your pain.

I know that this kind of season can feel like it may go on forever. No matter how long it lasts, I am here for you.

Even more important in this season, your Good Shepherd will be with you every minute of every day.

> The LORD Himself will go before you.
> He will be with you;
> He will not leave you or forget you.
> Don't be afraid and don't worry.
> DEUTERONOMY 31:8 NCV

The Shepherd promises
to lead us by the still waters...

...and the lively ones too!

Waves of hope and peace
on your ride of faith in Him.

The Shepherd Will Watch Over You

I often think about the many externals our Good Shepherd tends to, but, my friend, no one knows our heart, our soul, or our deepest desires better than He does—and, in my case, I love that you're a close second!

The Shepherd's eyes are aware of our circumstances; His heart is aware of our hurts, fears, and concerns.

The Shepherd protects us in this world; He heals the wounds in our private world.

He is in the still waters, and He is in the raging rapids.

We can count on Him—and I'm grateful I can count on you too.

A Note from Martha based on Luke 10:38–42:

I was so frustrated with my sister today. We had guests, hungry guests, and someone had to fix the meal. Of course I would have preferred sitting with her at Jesus' feet, but people would soon want to eat. Couldn't she help me for a few more minutes?

Then a loving word from my Lord cut through my frenzied activities, my frenzied heart. His wisdom? "All would be well if I actually treated the most important priority in my life—my relationship with Jesus—as the most important aspect of my life."

Yes, feeding those people I love is a joy and a necessity, but more important is feeding my soul as I spend time with my Good Shepherd, listen to His voice, bask in His presence. I want to make this the most precious priority in my day—and not just as a commitment in my heart, but as real-life actions. If I choose each day to spend time with Jesus, I will be able to approach the rest of my life with less stress and with an awareness of His presence with me. —Martha based on Luke 10:38–42

I'm praying, my friend, that you'll find peace for your heart and your day as you spend time with Jesus. May your joy in His presence be your strength for the tasks of your day.

The LORD says,
"I will make you wise and show you where to go.
I will guide you and watch over you."
PSALM 32:8 NCV

You Make a Difference

Imagine as you walk down the pasture trail, sheep are lined up on both sides waiting for a glimpse of you! Look! There she is! You hear "Bravo!" and "Encore!" Members of the crowd want selfies with you....

That may be fun to imagine, but I know your heart. The Shepherd's "Well done!" will mean more to you than any heavenly headlines or paparazzi. You touch so many people just by being you! I'm so blessed to call you my friend!

Think about living life for your Audience of One and hear what He has to say about that.

Sometimes people won't notice your efforts or give you recognition for something you've done. The credit may even go to someone else. Do it anyway, AS UNTO ME, for I will honor your obedience.

There may be times when you do your very best but your efforts fail. You may give sacrificially of your time or money to help someone and not receive even a simple "Thank you!" Do it anyway, AS UNTO ME, for I am your reward.

At times, keeping your word means giving up something you value, and keeping a commitment means personal sacrifice. Do it anyway, AS UNTO ME, for I do not withhold anything from you that is good.

You may speak the truth in love to others only to be rejected. You may do something with good intentions and be completely misunderstood. Do it anyway, AS UNTO ME, for I know your heart.

On occasion you will forgive others, only to have them hurt you again. Or you may reach out to bless others only to have them take advantage of your kindness. Do it anyway, AS UNTO ME, for I am your Friend.

May the Shepherd's blessings be yours in abundance as you continue to do all that you do as unto Him.

The LORD your God has chosen you
to be His own special treasure.
DEUTERONOMY 7:6 NLT

We
may feel
alone, but
the truth
is...

...the shepherd is always with us.

Praying He encourages your heart today!

Never Ever Alone

Our precious Shepherd brought us together for many reasons.

I think of the joy, the hope, the wisdom, the prayers, and the love you pour into my life.

I think another reason He brought us together is so we never feel alone. We can know in our heads that the Shepherd is always there for us. But sometimes we need wool and hooves to make our Shepherd's love more real.

Thanks for doing that for me.

Of course the Good Shepherd knew you first, and knows you best, and loves you even more than I do—and I love you a lot!

Once, before the foundation of the world, Jesus and His Father had a conversation about Their great plan of redemption—of bringing God's people back into relationship with Him—and that conversation included you. Jesus looked down the corridors of time and knew that you would be born. He saw your need for the forgiveness of sin and reconciliation with your heavenly Father, so He said to His Father, "I will go."

At the time His Father chose—and in an overwhelming expression of love—Jesus left heaven and came to earth so that He could be with you always. You were on His heart when He left His home in heaven. When He stretched out His hands on the cross, He showed you the extent of His love. When He returned to His Father, He began preparing an eternal home for you.

You are one of the beloved sheep He came to shepherd, to guide, to feed, to protect, to shelter, and to carry. You are one He calls His very own. You, my friend, have an amazing Friend in Jesus.

God has said,
"I will never leave you;
I will never abandon you."
HEBREWS 13:5 NCV

From the
SHEPHERD'S HEART
and mine...

Love, joy, peace &
ENCOURAGEMENT
to you!

P.S.
Oh, yes —
and my prayers too!

The Shepherd Is So Good to Us

I've been walking through the meadow, thinking about how good our Shepherd is—and thinking that you must have learned a lot from Him about how to be a friend.

The Good Shepherd helps me learn from yesterday and face the challenges of today. Knowing that He cares gives me peace. Walking with Him through life gives me joy.

I delight in all the good things He gives, including you who helps me learn from yesterday, face today's challenges, have peace, and live with joy!

Know what? Yes, you already know this: I'm not the only one thinking of you today. Of course your Good Shepherd is. And He is saying these things to you—and me:

- With Me, all things are possible.
- I will not fail you: trust Me. And know I am pleased when I see your faith.
- I am your Provider. Nothing that is good will be withheld from you.
- I am for you—so who can be against you?
- You are My child, and your times are in My hands.
- I will teach you and instruct you; I will guide you.
- Rest in My love.
- I will love you with an everlasting love.
- I will bless you so that you can be a blessing to others.
- I will never leave you or forsake you. I will be with you always.
- I'm preparing an eternal home for you.
- Your prayers to Me are sweet like incense.

I love you dearly!

—Your Good Shepherd
(And I love you, too, precious friend!)

*I love you...you bring me joy
and make me proud of you.*
PHILIPPIANS 4:1 NCV

Today is perfect for
JOY BAKING...

CUPCAKING...

and
CELEBRATING
YOU!

A Recipe for Good Times

Have you noticed that the Shepherd always cooks up something good whenever you and I are together?

Fun times, special memories, heart-to-heart talks—I love being with you more than I love butterscotch, peppermint, and even chocolate!

We need to get together soon!!! I know a great place for coffee and brownies!

There's a beautiful recipe for love in Ephesians 4 ESV that begins with the call to walk "with all humility and gentleness, with patience, bearing with one another in love...eager to maintain the unity of the Spirit in the bond of peace" (Ephesians 4:1–3 ESV).

Next we add some "Speaking the truth in love" just as our Good Shepherd does (v. 15).

Then we embrace our new life in Christ by putting off our old self and being renewed in the spirit of our minds (vv. 22–23).

The recipe ends with truths to help us love better, stronger, and deeper:

Speak the truth (v. 25).
Be angry (only in a healthy way, not letting it lead us to sin), but don't dwell in it unnecessarily ("do not let the sun go down on your anger") (v. 26).
Speak good things to each other (v. 29).
Get rid of negativity! Put away bitterness, rage, anger, harsh words, slander, and malice (v. 31).
Be kind and tenderhearted to each other (v. 32).
And be forgiving (v. 32).

"Let all bitterness and wrath and anger and clamor and slander be put away from you, along with all malice. Be kind to one another, tenderhearted, forgiving one another, as God in Christ forgave you" (Ephesians 4:32 ESV).

Thank You, Good Shepherd, for the Ephesians 4 guidance that helps us grow in love for You and for others.

A sweet friendship refreshes the soul.
PROVERBS 27:9 THE MESSAGE

It's a great mystery
HOW the Shepherd created
heaven and earth...

...but it's no wonder WHY.

He wanted a place where you could thrive in the life He planned for you... and you do just that!

Breathe In...Breathe Out

Taking time to smell the roses,
watch a butterfly,
nap on the grass...
and spend time together—
we need to do things like this more often.

When can we get together to slow down, relax,
and savor the wonder of the Shepherd's goodness
and grace in our lives, to savor the goodness and
grace of this friendship?

Have you ever gone outside at night to lie on the grass and gaze up at the heavens? The stars we see only hint at all God has created. With high-powered telescopes, astronomers are now able to look light-years out into the cosmos—and an aptly named light-year refers to the distance that light can travel in one year. (That's 5.88 trillion miles.)

Also, scientists now estimate that there are as many stars in the sky as there are grains of sand on all the beaches in the world! And a single handful of sand is estimated to have about 10,000 grains of sand. Only our omnipotent God could create trillions upon trillions of stars out there—and He even has a name for each of them! (Psalm 147:4).

Now think about the very busy third day of creation. Genesis 1:9–13 tells us that God gathered the water together in one place, let dry ground appear, and spoke into existence all the plants, trees, and other vegetation. Not a bad day's work!

Our God is amazing...and He knows a lot about getting good things done! Good things like making us friends!

> Long before He laid down
> earth's foundations,
> He had us in mind.
> EPHESIANS 1:4 THE MESSAGE

I've asked
the Shepherd
to bless you
TODAY...

...so expect
a "loaves and fishes"
kind of day!

Be BLeSSeD!*

Here Come the Blessings— Again!

Or is it still?

The Shepherd sure loves to bless His sheep! And He isn't satisfied with, so to speak, just a couple of rolls and a small fish.

He loves to bless us so much that we have leftovers! You know, those leftovers make it easier for us to be a blessing to others...which has been His plan all along!

We are blessed to be a blessing. Know that you are a blessing to me!

"Andrew, Simon Peter's brother, spoke up. 'There's a young boy here with five barley loaves and two fish. But what good is that with this huge crowd?'

'Tell everyone to sit down,' Jesus said. So they all sat down on the grassy slopes. (The men alone numbered 5,000.) Then Jesus took the loaves, gave thanks to God, and distributed them to the people. Afterward he did the same with the fish. And they all ate as much as they wanted. After everyone was full, Jesus told His disciples, 'Now gather the leftovers, so that nothing is wasted.' So they picked up the pieces and filled twelve baskets with scraps left by the people who had eaten from the five barley loaves" (John 6:8-13 NLT).

Imagine being there, in a huge crowd—perhaps more than 15,000—of hot, sweaty, hungry people. The disciples were getting concerned: "What are we going to do?"

In the face of this "impossible" situation, Jesus told all the people to sit down. Then He simply thanked God for the young boy's lunch. The disciples passed out the food—and kept passing it out until "everyone was full" of what just might have been the best meal they'd ever eaten!

And then there were all the leftovers afterward! What a great picture of blessings overflowing!

Jesus, our Shepherd, wants to bless you too. When His blessings overflow in your life, ask Him what He wants you do with it that would give Him glory.

Blessings overflow! Your goodness and unfailing kindness shall be with me all of my life.
PSALM 23:5–6 TLB

Even when we're under
the weather...

...we're covered by love
in the Shepherd's arms.

· · · · · · · · · ·

Praying You'll Be Strengthened
in His Care Today

No Better Place to Be

Our Shepherd speaks some wonderful words to us. And His Book teaches and encourages and blesses in so many ways.

But sometimes rather than speaking to us through words from either His Book or His undershepherds, our Shepherd just picks us up and holds us tightly in His arms.

When it's my turn to be held, I always feel so loved and cared for. I can simply rest in His arms—and I hope you make time to do some of that today, too, precious friend.

You're in the Shepherd's care.

I will be your God through all your lifetime…. I made you and I will care for you (Isaiah 46:4 TLB).

You're in the Shepherd's thoughts.

I can't even count how many times a day Your thoughts turn toward me (Psalm 139:18 TLB).

You're in the Shepherd's heart.

We know how much God loves us because…we believe Him when He tells us that He loves us dearly (I John 4:16 TLB).

You're in the Shepherd's hands.

I will strengthen you; I will help you; I will uphold you with My victorious right hand (Isaiah 41:10 TLB).

I am praying for you to know the Good Shepherd's presence with you and His power to strengthen and refresh you, to give you rest and health.

Our God, who is full of kindness through Christ,
will give you His eternal glory.
He personally will come and pick you up,
and set you firmly in place, and make you
stronger than ever.
I PETER 5:10 TLB

You're officially declared
"queen of the flock" today—
but you're always royalty in
the Shepherd's eyes.

Your Highness!

You Are Royalty!

So what do you want to do today, Your Royal Highness?

Want to frolic in the field?

Go down by the stream?

Visit some sheep in the meadow next door?

Shop for sweaters?

Maybe just spend some time lying under the willow tree, enjoying all the blessings of our Good Shepherd?

He sure does think you're special—and I do too!

Daughter of the King! Think about that phrase, that title, that privilege!

You can walk confidently, knowing who you are and whose you are.

God loves you.
He has good plans for you.
He created you to fulfill those plans.
He made you one-of-a-kind and wonderful.

And the fact that you are the King's daughter is evident in your warm ways, contagious joy, strong and ever-growing faith, fearlessness regarding the future, and Christlike love for the people blessed to know you and even those who momentarily, temporarily cross your path.

No jewel or gem could ever outsparkle the beauty of Jesus within you.

What a blessing, Your Royal Highness, to know you as a fellow princess and my cherished friend!

You are a chosen people.
You are royal priests, a holy nation,
God's very own possession. As a result,
you can show others the goodness of God,
for He called you out of the darkness
into His wonderful light.
1 PETER 2:9 NLT

Everlasting

I found these truths in the Shepherd's Book. I hope they encourage you, my friend, as much as they encouraged me.

You are My child.
Your times are in My hands.
My thoughts toward you are precious.
I will bless you.
I have placed My hand upon you.
I hold you with My hand.
I do everything for you in love.
I am for you.
I will not fail you.
I am your provider.
With Me, all things are possible!
I will love you with an everlasting love.

—Your Good Shepherd

Some things haven't changed and will never change. God's promises, for instance, are still in effect and always will be.

God is still the Author of history and the One who keeps the planets in their orbits. His plans will not fail. His purposes will not falter. His kingdom will not be defeated.

He came for us as a babe, He is coming again as the triumphant King, and an ultimate, eternal victory will be His in the end.

God is still on the throne, the Holy Spirit is still the Comforter, and Jesus, our Good Shepherd, still loves you!

May the promises of God and His unfailing love for you bring you true peace now and always. And may He continue to bless this friendship He has so graciously given us.

I love you!

Let's keep a firm grip
on the promises that keep us going.
He always keeps His word.
HEBREWS 10:23 THE MESSAGE

...AND THAT'S REASON

FOR CELEBRATION!

God looked over everything
He had made;
it was so good, so very good!

GENESIS 1:31 THE MESSAGE

Glimpses of His Glory

Sometimes life can feel repetitive—we wake up, say "Good morning" to the Shepherd, eat, play, roam, and nap. But when you're around, things seem brighter, smiles and laughter overtake us, and before you know it we're running around having a grand ol' time!

There is something about routine that the Shepherd likes. After all, He created us to go to sleep every day...and wake up too! So why do we feel like we're in "a rut" sometimes?

I suppose without the routine our lives would be a hundred times more chaotic than they already are! I think part of it is that God likes faithfulness. Over and over, day after day, He gives us another chance to glimpse His glory hidden in the routine and witness His faithfulness time after time. We learn to look to Him and count on Him for His unfailing friendship right in the middle of wherever we are.

And that's how I see you, too. Your friendship to me is a daily glimpse of God's goodness, a sweet reminder that He sees and knows me and loves me, too. It never gets old! You are a picture of grace—God's amazing gift to this world and to me. I'm so grateful that you're in this journey with me, walking with our Shepherd, right by my side!

> If we are faithless,
> he remains faithful—
> for he cannot deny himself.
> II TIMOTHY 2:13 ESV

It's easy to get
carried away
when it comes to

CELEBRATING
YOU!

(the Shepherd
is rejoicing too!)

Is that a joyous
choir I hear?
No, it is the Lord Himself
exulting over you in happy song.
ZEPHANIAH 3:17 TLB

The Real Deal

With you, I'm at home. You are safe, trustworthy, and a tremendously good listener. And at just the right time you help me remember the Shepherd, who stays by my side.

I thank God for you every day because you don't run from my struggles and pain. Instead, you remind me that His strength overcomes all battles. This world can be tough, but you always find a way to guide me back to the Light. And for that, I will be forever grateful.

Loyalty seems like a lost art these days. Affection and fandom rise and fall faster than the noon and evening tides, and it's hard to know who's the real deal. Probably the best proof happens through the hard times. When life isn't going well and your world feels like it's falling apart, true friends rally around you and stay the course.

God says real friendship—the kind His Spirit brings—sticks closer than a brother. Stronger than blood ties, God's Spirit empowers His people to love like our Shepherd did, laying down our own lives to help and heal the wounded.

And you're that kind of friend to me! You help me get before the Lord Jesus when, because of weariness or discouragement, I can't do it on my own. I thank God for the good gift of your friendship!

A man of many companions
may come to ruin,
but there is a friend
who sticks closer than a brother.
PROVERBS 18:24 ESV

Friendship Promises and Blessings

Every time you cross my mind,
I break out in exclamations of thanks to God.
PHILIPPIANS 1:3 THE MESSAGE

God will be the bond between me and you.
I SAMUEL 20:42 THE MESSAGE

Thanking God over and over for you
is not only a pleasure; it's a must.
II THESSALONIANS 1:3 THE MESSAGE

Even before He made the world,
God loved us and chose us in Christ to be holy
and without fault in His eyes.
EPHESIANS 1:4 NLT

He closely attends to the prayers
of God-loyal people.
PROVERBS 15:29 THE MESSAGE

Oh, the joys of those who trust the LORD.
PSALM 40:4 NLT

The LORD your God has chosen you
to be His own special treasure.
DEUTERONOMY 7:6 NLT

I can never stop thanking God
for all the wonderful gifts He has given you.
I CORINTHIANS 1:4 TLB

My sheep listen to My voice;
I know them, and they follow Me....
No one can snatch them away from Me.
JOHN 10:27-28 NLT

And the Lord—who is the Spirit—
makes us more and more like Him
as we are changed into His glorious image
II CORINTHIANS 3:18 NLT

Keep on loving your friends;
do your work in welcoming hearts.
PSALM 36:10 THE MESSAGE

He calls His own sheep by name.
JOHN 10:3 NLT

For you have a special place in my heart.
You share with me the special favor of God.
PHILIPPIANS 1:7 NLT

God...has blessed us with every blessing
in heaven because we belong to Christ.
EPHESIANS 1:3 TLB

*I will be your God through all your lifetime....
I made you and I will care for you.
I will carry you along and be your Savior.*
ISAIAH 46:4 TLB

May you be blessed by the LORD.
PSALM 115:15 NLT

May God our Father shower you
with blessings and fill you with His great peace.
COLOSSIANS 1:2 TLB

Your love has given me much joy.
PHILEMON 1:7 NLT

The eyes of the LORD
watch over those who do right,
and His ears are open
to their prayers.
1 PETER 3:12 NLT

His radiance exceeds anything in earth and sky;
He's built a monument—His very own people!
PSALM 148:13–14 THE MESSAGE

Share each other's burdens,
and in this way obey the law of Christ.
GALATIANS 6:2 NLT

Try to realize what this means—
the Lord is God!
He made us—we are His people,
the sheep of His pasture.
PSALM 100:3 TLB

Let Him have all your worries and cares,
for He is always thinking about you
and watching everything that concerns you.
I PETER 5:7 TLB

Two are better than one
because they have a good return
for their labor.
ECCLESIASTES 4:9 NASB

We who had sweet fellowship together.
PSALM 55:14 NASB

Better is a neighbor who is near
than a brother far away.
PROVERBS 27:10 NASB

A sweet friendship refreshes the soul.
PROVERBS 27:9 THE MESSAGE

A friend loves at all times.
PROVERBS 17:17 NASB

Faithful are the wounds of a friend.
PROVERBS 27:6 NASB

There is a friend who sticks closer than a brother.
PROVERBS 18:24 NASB

O magnify the LORD with me,
and let us exalt His name together.
PSALM 34:3 NASB

Every perfect gift is from above.
JAMES 1:17 NASB

God cares...right down to the last detail.
JAMES 5:11 THE MESSAGE

I pray that God, the source of hope,
will fill you completely with joy and peace
because you trust in Him.
Then you will overflow with confident hope
through the power of the Holy Spirit.
ROMANS 15:13 NLT

The LORD Himself will go before you.
He will be with you;
He will not leave you or forget you.
Don't be afraid and don't worry.
DEUTERONOMY 31:8 NCV

I love you...you bring me joy
and make me proud of you.
PHILIPPIANS 4:1 NCV

Let all bitterness and wrath and anger
and clamor and slander be put away from you,
along with all malice.
Be kind to one another, tenderhearted,
forgiving one another,
as God in Christ forgave you.
EPHESIANS 4:31–32 ESV

We know how much God loves us because...
we believe Him when He tells us
that He loves us dearly.
I JOHN 4:16 TLB

Our God, who is full of kindness through Christ,
will give you His eternal glory.
He personally will come and pick you up,
and set you firmly in place,
and make you stronger than ever.
I PETER 5:10 TLB

You are a chosen people. You are royal priests,
a holy nation, God's very own possession.
As a result, you can show others
the goodness of God,
for He called you out of the darkness
into His wonderful light.
I PETER 2:9 NLT

Dear Friend,

This book was prayerfully crafted with you, the reader, in mind—every word, every sentence, every page—was thoughtfully written, designed, and packaged to encourage you...right where you are this very moment. At DaySpring, our vision is to see every person experience the life-changing message of God's love. So, as we worked through rough drafts, design changes, edits and details, we prayed for you to deeply experience His unfailing love, indescribable peace, and pure joy. It is our sincere hope that through these Truth-filled pages your heart will be blessed, knowing that God cares about you—your desires and disappointments, your challenges and dreams.

He knows. He cares. He loves you unconditionally.

BLESSINGS!
THE DAYSPRING BOOK TEAM